UNBELIEVABLE RANDOM FACTS

For Inquisitive Kids

By Melanie Cartwright

D1114425

Table of Contents

Read Me First!

I have a few things to tell you!!

Did you know that playing the didgeridoo can help cure sleep apnea? Or that an ostrich's eye is bigger than its brain? You read that right! This book is filled with facts that you didn't even know that you needed to know. These facts will make you the cool kid on the block whippin' out fabulous factoids to break the ice with shy strangers and curmudgeon family members. Keep yourself enthralled on those boring car rides or flights with hundreds of totally random and mind-blowing facts.

Nevertheless, there's a few things you should know. First of all, there are no rules in this book. You can read it from the first page to the last, last page to the first, or you can skip around and read the parts that interest you the most. Furthermore, please feel free to highlight, dog-ear, write notes, or even doodle in this book. Bet you can't do that to a TikTok video! This is a real, physical book a rarity these days, so I encourage you to take full advantage of its tactile benefits.

Check it out and check it off!

Each fact in this book comes with two empty dots. You can decide how you want to use the dots. For example: Did you already know that fact? Check it off! Is that fact super cool and you want to do more research on that fact? Check it off! Do you want to remember to quiz your mom or dad on that fact later? Check it off! You can even check off with different colors. A green checkmark can be a fact you know to be true and an orange checkmark can be a fact you doubt. You can use different symbols such as a checkmark, an x or simply fill in the circle. Get creative! You get to choose what each empty dot means and then check it off to come back to later. Make this book your own so that you get the most out of it.

Find Out More!

This book is intended to spark curiosity. Please don't read this book and ask no questions. At the end of some sections, I provide a few resources if you want to know more about a given topic. I encourage you to further investigate any fact that catches your eye.

Proceed at your own risk, this book contains facts gathered from a variety of sources. This book's main purpose is to entertain and spark curiosity.   It is not to be taken as a strict adherence to the truth. The author hopes that all facts contained in this book are all true, however, misinformation, unfortunately, is the bane of the new millennium. Thus, I cannot guarantee that everything is true.

In addition, some facts are time-sensitive and subject to change. The population of a country does not stay stagnant and scientists change their minds. For example, Pluto used to be a planet when the author was a kid. (I know that must have been a long time ago) Good scientists and researchers maintain an open mind and are always willing to look at new evidence. I encourage the reader to do their own research and verify any facts that interest you.

>Whew< Ok that's it! Enjoy!

○ ○ There are currently over 7,000 languages in the world.

○ ○ The majority of the world speaks more than one language, 40% of the world's population is bilingual (able to speak two languages) and almost 20% speak more than two languages. Only 40% of the world is monolingual (able to speak one language). How many languages do you speak?

○ ○ The country with the most languages is Papua New Guinea with 839 languages.

○ ○ There is no universal sign language, instead there are over 300 different sign languages used in different countries and regions around the world. For example, British Sign Language (BSL) is a completely different language from ASL or American Sign Language. Someone who knows ASL will not understand BSL the same way someone who speaks English doesn't understand someone who speaks Vietnamese.

○ ○ The oldest written language is Sumerian dating back to 3500 B.C. Spoken in ancient Mesopotamia, present-day southern Iraq, it was gradually replaced by other languages and is related to no living languages today.

○ ○ Language with the shortest alphabet, Rotokas, spoken in Papua New Guinea, has only twelve letters.

○ ○ The language with the longest alphabet is Khmer, sometimes called Cambodian, with 74 characters. An alphabet is a set of letters or symbols used to represent a sound or a relative sound in spoken language.

○ ○ The language with the most distinct sounds or phonemes is Taa, spoken in Botswana and Namibia.

○ ○ Pirahã and Rotokas tie for the least amount of phonemes at eleven each. Pirahã is a language spoken by a tribe in the Amazon in Brazil.

○ ○ The language with the most consonants is Ubykh which has 84 phonemic (distinct) consonants, but only 3 phonemic vowels. The last speaker of Ubykh died in 1992.

○ ○ Danish has the most distinct vowels with 27 and 19 diphthongs (two vowels said together as one).

○ ○ Some English accents will have a slightly different number of vowel sounds, but generally speaking, English has around 20 distinct vowel sounds, despite only having five vowel letters in its alphabet.

○ ○ While Cantonese (spoken in Hong Kong and Southern China) is said to have six tones, several Kam-Sui languages of southern China have nine contrastive tones. A tone is when you use pitch (such as high or low) to change the meaning. For example, the Kam language has 3 fixed tones (high, mid, and low); 2 raising tones, 2 falling tones, a dipping tone, and a peaking tone.

○ ○ The most common word order is Subject Object Verb (i.e. The cat the mouse ate.), in fact, they are the majority. 56% of world languages have SOV word order. Only 13% of languages are Subject Verb Object word order like English.

○ ○ Bahasa Indonesian uses reduplication (or repetition) for plurals (nouns that are more than one). For example, "student" is *murid* and *murid-murid* means "students."

○ ○ Quechua (spoken in South America by over 7 million people) has two pronouns for "we". There is inclusive "you and me" *noqancheq* and exclusive "me and not you" *noqayku*. Can you think of a situation that might come in handy?

○ ○ A native speaker of a language will know 15,000-20,000 lemmas or word families in their first language. A lemma is a root word. Some languages will have more words in the dictionary, but the average speaker of any given language will have about the same working vocabulary.

○ ○ All languages are acquired at the same rate. Thus, no language is "harder" or "easier" than another from the point of view of a newborn baby. It's only when you have already acquired one language that it is harder to learn a very different language as an adult. For example, a baby will learn Spanish or Chinese at the same rate, but a Spanish-speaking adult will learn Italian faster than it would learn Chinese because Italian is related and thus more similar to Spanish while Chinese is not.

○ ○ African American Vernacular English (AAVE) has a meaning distinction similar to the Spanish verbs to be "ser" and "estar". For example, "She late." means she's late now, and "She be late." means "She's frequently late."

Did you know??

English has added 3 new ways to introduce speech or say "say":

1. Then, Bob's all "No way!"
2. So, Charlie goes "Yes way!"
3. Finally, Dave's like "Seriously?"

How many of these do you use?

○ ○ Languages are always changing. Through each generation, new words are invented or borrowed, old words' meanings evolve and pronunciations shift. Ask your grandma and grandpa how their language has changed!

○ ○ English has lost the distinction between "wh" and "w". Older generations could tell "which witch is which", however, many younger generations of English speakers cannot. Can you tell which witch is which?

3

○ ○ In Guugu Yimithirr, an aboriginal language spoken in Australia, all the directions used are cardinal directions. Cardinal directions are North, South, East, West, and the directions in between. They don't have words for left, right, front, or back.

○ ○ English is not a Romance language descended from Latin. English has strong Germanic roots and is closer grammatically to German than its Romance language counterparts like Spanish or Italian.

○ ○ English is distantly related to languages like Urdu (spoken in Pakistan) and Farsi (spoken in Iran). English belongs to the Germanic language family that is part of the bigger Indo-European family. Another branch of the Indo-European language family tree is the Indo-Iranian branch which Urdu and Farsi belong to.

○ ○ Some languages have a dual grammatical number, in addition to singular and plural. When a noun or pronoun appears in dual form, it refers to precisely two of the objects identified by the noun or pronoun acting as a single unit or in unison. So, if you are counting sheep in Slovenian (spoken in Slovenia) you would say "one sheep" *ena ovca*, "two sheep" *dve ovci*, "three sheep" *tri ovce*.

Find out more!

Visit Ethnologue

https://www.ethnologue.com/

Or World Atlas of Language Structures

https://wals.info/

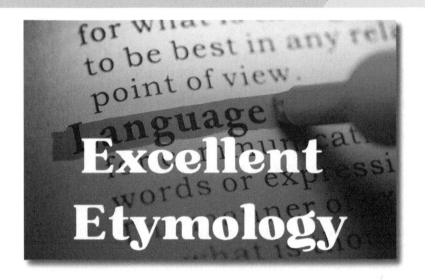

○ ○ Etymology is the study of the origin of words and the way in which their meanings have changed.

Nightmare

○ ○ Contrary to the way it sounds, the "mare" in "nightmare" does not come from female horse. Instead it comes from Germanic folklore, in which a "mare" is an evil female spirit that sits on a sleeping person's chest, suffocating them or giving them bad dreams.

Sandwich

○ ○ What do you do if you are playing cards and get hungry? Why ask your butler to put some beef between two pieces of bread. This is what the 4th Earl of Sandwich did. His fellow card players thought it was so ingenious that they started asking for "same as Sandwich" and the rest, as they say, is history.

Quarantine

○ ○ The word, quarantine comes from the Venetian dialect form of the Italian words "quaranta giorni", or "forty days". This is because ships had to be isolated for forty days before anyone on board could enter Venice in order to prevent the spread of the plague.

Malaria

○ ○ You might be able to guess this word's origin. It comes from the Italian "mal" meaning "bad" and "aria" meaning "air". It was once thought that Malaria was transmitted through "bad air" from the swamps near Rome.

Clue

○ ○ Here's a *clue* as to the origins of the word "clue." It originally meant "ball of yarn" in ancient Greek. Still stumped? In Greek mythology, Ariadne, a Cretan princess, gives Theseus, a mythical king, a ball of yarn to help him find his way out of the Minotaur's labyrinth. Theseus unraveled the yarn behind him as he went into the maze so that he could work his way back out in reverse. As a result, the word "clue" came to mean something that helps you figure out the way.

Hazard

○ ○ Did you know we get the word "hazard" from 13th-century Arabic? The word comes from *al-zahr* which were dice used in various gambling games. Since gambling is precarious, and it was also risky that con men might use weighted dice, the dice became synonymous with anything high risk, e.g. "dicey".

Ketchup

○ ○ This word started out as *kôe-chiap* or *kê-chiap* in the Chinese Amoy dialect for a sauce of pickled fish and spices. However, before it came into English, the sauce became popular in modern-day Singapore and Malaysia known as *kecap*, pronounced, "kay-chap". It was there where British explorers discovered the delicious sauce we enjoy today.

Salary

○ ○ In Ancient Egypt, laborers were paid with salt because they could use it to preserve their food. The Roman Empire continued using this form of payment and it took on the name "salary" for "that which was given to workers at the end of the working month."

Nice

○ ○ Linguists trace the word "nice" to Old French where it referred to people who were ridiculously overdressed. Eventually, it came to mean someone who was "nicely" or sophisticatedly dressed and finally someone who was refined or sophisticated.

Shampoo

○ ○ Ever have a *chapati* when eating Indian food and think about washing your hair? Well, incredibly, these two words share the same root! The word shampoo comes from Hindi and means 'to massage'. Derived from the Sanskrit root *chapati*, the word initially referred to any type of pressing, kneading, or soothing.

Mortgage

○ ○ Have you asked your parents whether they want a death pledge? In French, the word *mort* means "dead" and *gage* means "pledge" — so yes, "mortgage" basically means "death pledge." But fear not! It was actually called this because the debt ends — or becomes "dead" — when the pledge is fulfilled.

Sarcasm

○ ○ Ever hear a sarcastic remark and think "that tears flesh like a dog?" The word "sarcasm" actually comes from the Greek verb *sarkazein*, which literally means "to tear flesh like dogs." Eventually, it also came to mean to "gnash teeth" and "to speak bitterly."

Tragedy

○ ○ Linguists are still scratching their heads over this one. The word "tragedy" originates from the Greek word *tragoidia*, which literally means "goat song." Some linguists theorize it's because Ancient Greeks used to dress in goatskins and others postulate that goats were often given out as prizes at Greek plays or sometimes even sacrificed.

Muscle

○ ○ Ever think that it looked like there were little mice running under your skin? The word "muscle" comes from the Latin word musculus, which translates to "little mouse." because people thought the movement and shape of the muscles looked like little mice!

Tulip

○ ○ Did you think this word came from "two lips"? Surprisingly, we get this word from the Turkish word *tülbent*, which means "turban". Do you think the shape of a tulip looks like a turban?

Jumbo

○ ○ Jumbo was the name of a six-ton elephant at the London Zoo in the 19th century. His name lives on in our language as anything that is "extremely large."

Robot

○ ○ The word "robot" comes from a 1920's Czech play. The word comes from the old Church Slavonic word *robota*, meaning "servitude," and in the play it describes mechanical workers who "lack nothing but a soul."

Vaccine

○ ○ Can you believe we get this word from cows? British physician Edward Jenner prevented smallpox by injecting people with the similar but much milder cowpox virus (variolae vaccinae). So he called it a vaccine.

Find Out More!

Visit the Oxford English Dictionary:

www.oed.com

MOTHERLY MAYHEM

○ ○ Skink moms will eat up their eggs if they think a predator will get them. Skink moms stink!

○ ○ Female cuckoos will lay their eggs in another bird's nest so that they don't have to raise their chicks.

○ ○ House sparrow moms will seek out the nests of other females who have mated with her partner and kill the their chicks.

○ ○ Mama pandas often give birth to twins, however, they often abandon the weaker one and only raise one baby.

○ ○ Opposite of a panda mom, if a mama black bear gives birth to only one cub, she might abandon it. By her logic, raising one cub is almost as much work as raising two or three, so it's not worth it to raise only one.

○ ○ Mother rabbits leave their babies alone almost instantly after giving birth. They check in on the burrow briefly once a day.

○ ○ Mother hamsters will actually eat some of their babies. If they have more babies than they can raise, then they will eat the extra ones.

○ ○ Dracula ants don't kill or eat their babies, but they will drink their blood!

○ ○ Lioness mothers will allow a new leader of the pride to kill their young. This is because lionesses want to pass on the genes of the strongest lion, not that of a dethroned king.

○ ○ The hooded grebe mother will lay two eggs but only takes care of the first chick to hatch. She will leave the second egg for the chick to hatch all alone.

○ ○ Black eagle moms let their chicks duke it out in a Hunger Games-style match. Black eagle chicks often fight to the death while mama eagles watch on and don't intervene.

○ ○ Harp seal moms leave their pups at 2 weeks. However, the pups aren't ready to swim until they are about 8 weeks old! So they stay in the same spot and try not to get eaten! Unfortunately, only about a third of the pups survive.

Want a snack?

Burying beetle moms will eat their babies if they bug their moms too much! Researchers think that this is because the beetle moms believe the strong babies only ask for food when they are truly hungry. Think about that next time you want a snack before dinner!

Magnificent Moms

○ ○ Alligator moms make their nests out of rotting plants. This compost creates heat to warm the eggs so that mama alligator doesn't have to sit on the eggs all day.

○ ○ Elephant moms are pregnant for 22 months. That's almost two years! And their babies can weigh up to 200 pounds!

○ ○ Empire penguin moms lay the eggs but then leave the eggs to the penguin dads while they travel up to 50 miles to go get food.

○ ○ Mama koalas chew their own poop to feed it to their baby joeys! Koalas eat eucalyptus leaves that only adult koalas can digest.

○ ○ An octopus mom, called a hen, lays up to 200,000 eggs.

○ ○ Red horn-billed moms will seal themselves to their nests with poop and mud to protect their eggs from predators.

○ ○ Mama giraffes only sleep a total of 30 minutes a day as they stand guard to protect their babies.

○ ○ Mama cats, called queens, have a special noise or "chirrup" that they use to call their kittens. Have you heard this sound?

○ ○ Orangutang moms keep their babies close to them for up to eight years.

○ ○ Mother hens are constantly turning their eggs, up to five times an hour. They will cluck to their eggs and sometimes, the chicks, from inside the egg, will chirp back!

○ ○ Harp seal moms lose seven pounds a day while nursing their pups. Their pups gain five pounds a day.

○ ○ Mama polar bears sleep through the whole birth process. They give birth during hibernation.

○ ○ Polar bear moms often give birth to twins. They also put on up to 400 pounds.

○ ○ Mama blue whales produce up to fifty gallons of milk per day.

○ ○ Some earwig moms offer the ultimate sacrifice: themselves. Their babies will eat their mom after hatching.

○ ○ African wild dogs can give birth to up to 16 puppies in a single litter!

Marco! Polo!

Seal moms can recognize the voice of their babies out of thousands of seals. They will find each other by calling out back and forth like they are playing Marco Polo.

AWESOME HU-MOMS

○ ○ The longest human pregnancy ever recorded was 375 days. That's longer than a year!

○ ○ The heaviest baby ever recorded to be born was 22 pounds, born to Signora Carmelina Fedele in Aversa, Italy, in September 1955.

○ ○ Lina Medina, the world's youngest mother, gave birth when Lina was just 5 years and 7 months old in Peru in 1939.

○ ○ The oldest woman to give birth is Erramatti Mangayamma at age 73. She gave birth to twins in India in 2019.

○ ○ Halima Cisse, a 25-year-old mother from Mali, gave birth to the world's only known surviving nonuplets on May 4th, 2021 in Casablanca, Morocco. That's nine babies!

○ ○ Jayne Bleackley holds the record for the shortest interval between births at 208 days or 6 and a half months. She gave birth to a son on September 3, 1999. Later she gave birth to a daughter on March 30, 2000.

○ ○ Mrs. Feodor Vassilyev of Russia holds the record the biological mother of the most children. She gave birth to 69 children between 1725 and 1765.

∘ ∘ In the 1700s, mothers in the U.S. had an average of 7-10 children. In the 1950s mothers averaged 3-4 children. Nowadays, American moms have 2 kids on average. The world average is 2.3 children per woman.

∘ ∘ Unfortunately, around 800 women die every day from pregnancy-related causes during pregnancy, childbirth, and postpartum around the world.

∘ ∘ It is more dangerous to give birth in the U.S. than in 49 other countries, including Kuwait, Bulgaria, and South Korea.

∘ ∘ In the U.S., African American women are almost 4 times more likely to die during childbirth than their Caucasian counterparts.

∘ ∘ When hearing its mother's voice, a fetus' heart will beat faster.

∘ ∘ You started your life inside your grandmother! Female fetuses develop all the eggs they will ever have while inside the womb. Therefore, the egg that eventually became you was developed inside your grandmother's uterus.

How many babies were born in the time it took you to read this?

4.3 babies are born every second. That's 258 babies an hour and 6,192 babies a day

∘ ∘ Because one of the first utterances babies make is a "ma" sound, most languages around the world have that sound as the basis for their word for "mother." The word for "mom" is "mama" in Mandarin Chinese, "mamma" in Icelandic, "em" in Hebrew, and "me" in Vietnamese.

∘ ∘ In Ethiopia, families gather for several days in the fall to honor motherhood by singing songs and feasting.

○ ○ In Thailand, Mother's Day is celebrated on the birthday of the current queen, Sirikit, on August 12th.

○ ○ Mother's Day in the U.S. was originally proposed as a day women could protest against war. Julia Ward Howe, pacifist, and suffragette suggested Mother's Day in 1872 after the Civil War.

○ ○ Anna Jarvis, is responsible for making Mother's Day as we currently know it. Anna founded the Mother's Day International Association and persuaded Congress to recognize it as a national holiday. Anna even persuaded President Woodrow Wilson to declare it a federal holiday in 1914.

○ ○ Anna Jarvis, the same woman who championed Mother's Day, later tried to stop Mother's Day because she hated its commercialization.

○ ○ Wearing a white carnation on Mother's Day means that a person's mother has passed away. Wearing a colored carnation means that the person's mother is still living.

○ ○ More calls are made on Mother's Day than any other day of the year.

○ ○ The month, when most babies are born in the U.S., is August, and the day when most are born is Tuesday.

○ ○ Women who have their last child after 33 have twice the odds of living to the age of 95.

○ ○ In Canada, working moms get a yearlong leave and 55% of their salary during that first year after having a baby. In Cuba, new moms get 6 months of maternity leave with a full salary.

Father Facts

○ ○ The world's oldest father, Ramajit Raghav from India, was 96 years old when his wife gave birth to a baby boy.

○ ○ The youngest father in the world is a boy from China, who, at 9, had a child with an 8-year-old girl, in 1910.

○ ○ The father with the most children is most likely Ismail Ibn Sharif, an Alaouite sultan who fathered 888 children with hundreds of wives and concubines in the late 17th century.

○ ○ Many fathers experience couvade syndrome, also known as "sympathy pregnancy." This means they experience similar symptoms to the pregnant mothers such as vomiting and nausea.

○ ○ The number of stay-at-home dads has doubled in since the 1970s. SAH dads are defined as married fathers with children younger than 15 who have not worked at least one year to care for the family while their wives work outside of the home.

○ ○ A man who has many brothers is more likely to have sons. In contrast, a man who has many sisters is more likely to have daughters.

○ ○ Fathers over the age of 40 are significantly less likely to have sons.

○ ○ At least 66 countries guarantee a father's right to paid paternity leave, and at least 31 offer 14 weeks or more. The United States is not one of them.

○ ○ According to a new study, fathers who share household chores with their wives tend to have more ambitious daughters.

○ ○ A 4,000-year-old Babylonian tablet that a boy carved to wish his dad good health and long life is considered the world's oldest "Father's Day Card."

○ ○ Father's Day was first suggested in 1909 by Sonora Dodd to honor her father, a widowed Civil War veteran with six children.

○ ○ Father's Day did not become a federal holiday in the U.S. until 1972.

○ ○ Father's Day in Spain and Belgium is on March 19. In Australia and New Zealand, Father's day is in September. In Britain, Canada, and the U.S., it is in June.

> **Studies have shown that fathers of daughters live longer on average by 74 weeks per daughter born.**

DEVOTED DADS

○ ○ Seahorse dads carry and give birth to about 2,000 babies with each pregnancy Seahorse dads even experience contractions!

○ ○ A sea catfish dad will go for weeks without eating because he is holding the eggs in his mouth until they hatch.

○ ○ Arowana dads also carry eggs in their mouths until they hatch. Even after hatching, arowana dads continue to carry hatchlings in their mouths, letting them out only on occasion to swim and explore. If they swim too far, papa arowana will suck them back into his mouth.

○ ○ The South American Darwin frog dad doesn't just hold the eggs in his mouth. The Darwin frog actually swallows the eggs and holds them in his vocal sac (the stretchy skin underneath a frog's chin that expands when they ribbit). When the eggs are ready to hatch, he vomits them up.

○ ○ Midwife toad dads wrap strings of eggs around their hind limbs immediately after fertilization (hence the name 'Midwife Toad') and carry them until they are ready to hatch, then they place the eggs into a suitable pool for the tadpoles to hatch.

○ ○ Red fox fathers will bury food close to the den to help their pups learn how to sniff and forage for their food.

○ ○ A golden jackal dad will regurgitate his food to feed it to his babies.

○ ○ Jacana bird dads incubate the eggs and raise the chicks on their own. Jacana bird moms leave after laying their eggs.

○ ○ Wood-feeding cockroach dads will sweep their nurseries clean to protect their families from infection.

○ ○ A Namaqua sand grouse dad will fly as far as 50 miles a day in Africa's Kalahari Desert to soak himself in water and return to his nest so that his chicks can drink from his feathers.

○ ○ A Siamese fighting fish dad catches the eggs in his mouth as the mother lays them. Then he places the eggs in the bubble nest that he has prepared.

○ ○ Golden Lion Tamarin dads carry their infants on their backs all day for six to seven weeks, only taking a break when the mama tamarins nurse their babies.

○ ○ Father flamingos are very fair partners. They equally partake in selecting the nesting site, building the nests, incubating the eggs, and parenting the chicks.

○ ○ Father marmosets take their fatherly duties seriously, cleaning and watching their babies and carrying them to their mother only when babies need to be nursed.

> **Poison Dart Frog dads will pee on their eggs to prevent them from drying out.**

ASTOUNDING ANIMALS

○ ○ The shortest-living animal in the world is the mayfly. It only lives for twenty-four hours. What would you do if you only lived for a day?

○ ○ The Madagascar radiated tortoise is the longest verified living animal. One of them lived to the ripe old age of 188 years.

○ ○ The most venomous snake in the world, the inland taipan, can kill 100 fully grown men in less than 30 minutes.

○ ○ The world's deadliest animal is the mosquito. Mosquito-born diseases such as malaria, kill up to 750,000 people a year.

○ ○ The fastest animal is the peregrine falcon with a diving speed of 242 mph (389 kph).

○ ○ The fastest animal horizontally is the Brazilian free-tailed bat, which can reach speeds of 100 mph.

○ ○ The fastest swimmer is the black marlin which can swim up to 80 miles per hour or 128 kilometers per hour.

○ ○ The strongest bite in the world belongs to the Nile crocodile whose jaws can apply 5,000 pounds of pressure per square inch.

○ ○ A crocodile's bite is 10 times more powerful than that of a great white shark.

○ ○ The world's best jumper is the flea, which can jump 200 times its body length. They are able to jump 10 inches (25 cm) vertically and up to 18 inches (45 cm) horizontally. That is equal to a human jumping as high as the Empire State Building in New York.

○ ○ The howler monkey is as loud as a jet engine, making it the loudest land animal. The monkey's howls can be heard up to three miles away.

○ ○ The fastest recorded animal movement is the snap of the jaw of a blood "Dracula" ant. When it snaps its mandibles, it goes from 0 to 200mph in 0.000015 seconds. That's 5,000 times faster than a human blink.

○ ○ A blue whale's tongue weighs as much as one elephant.

○ ○ For each human, there are more than 1.4 billion insects. That's 11.2 quintillion total on the planet. A quintillion is one with 18 zeros!

○ ○ Ants have an estimated population of 20 quadrillions. (That's a one with 15 zeros.)

○ ○ There are an estimated 8.7 million species on Earth and more than 80% of them are undiscovered.

By the Numbers

1,000,000 = 1 million

1,000,000,000 = 1 billion

1,000,000,000,000 = 1 trillion

1,000,000,000,000,000 = 1 quadrillion

1,000,000,000,000,000,000 = 1 quintillion

Amazing Abilities

○ ○ A flamingo's head has to be upside down when it eats.

○ ○ Frogs can see in the back of them. A frog's visual range is 360 degrees.

○ ○ Otters will hold each other's hands or paws while sleeping so their mate doesn't float away.

○ ○ Hummingbirds can fly backward; the only birds that have this ability.

○ ○ The horned lizard shoots blood out of its own eyes. It can shoot blood up to three feet! If that doesn't scare the predator away, it can also puff up its body to twice its own size.

○ ○ Koalas will sleep for up to 22 hours a day. They need a lot of energy to digest their diet of eucalyptus leaves because the leaves contain a lot of toxins.

○ ○ Swifts can fly, without ever landing, for almost an entire year. They spend most of their lives in the air.

○ ○ A cockroach can survive weeks after having its head cut off.

○ ○ Mexican walking fish, or axolotl, can regrow the same limb up to 5 times, and even regenerate parts of its brain.

○ ○ An ostrich can kill a lion. Their legs are so powerful they can kill a lion with one kick!

○ ○ Tardigrades can go without eating for an entire decade. These microscopic animals that look like tiny bears can also endure extreme temperatures such as up to 300 and down to -457.6 degrees Fahrenheit.

○ ○ The Alaskan wood frog will literally freeze during the winter. Its heart will stop beating and the blood will stop pumping. After seven months, they hop back to life.

○ ○ While only the size of a paperclip, the golden poison dart frog can kill you with a single touch.

○ ○ The dung beetle can navigate by moonlight. They push their dung balls in a straight line using patterns created when moonlight interacts with particles in the atmosphere.

○ ○ Sharks can hunt using electricity! Fish movement sends out tiny electrical signals that the shark picks up on with a series of jelly-filled pores on their head. This is called electroreception.

How long can a snail sleep?

A. 30 hour naps

B. 2 month hibernation

C. Up to 3 years

Answer: 3 years

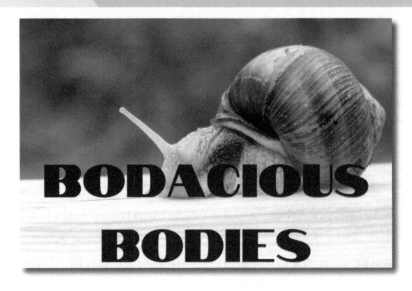

BODACIOUS BODIES

○ ○ Only half a dolphin's brain sleeps at a time.

○ ○ The animal with the most teeth in the world is the African giant snail with around 25,600. Even a common garden snail has 14,000 teeth.

○ ○ The teeth of an aquatic snail called the limpet are the strongest known biological material on Earth, even stronger than titanium.

○ ○ Dolphin's teeth have rings that grow each year, like a tree. You can tell how old a dolphin is by its teeth!

○ ○ Sharks lose about a tooth a week. That's a lot of tooth fairy money.

○ ○ Rodents such as squirrels and rabbits have teeth that never stop growing. They eat nuts and other hard things to wear them down.

○ ○ The longest canine teeth, at three feet, belong to hippopotamuses. Maybe we should call them hippo teeth instead of canines?

○ ○ Most animals don't get cavities. This is because most animals don't eat ice cream and donuts, or have diets high in sugar.

○ ○ Like baby humans who suck their thumbs, baby elephants suck their trunks for comfort.

○ ○ The Giant Pacific Octopus has 3 hearts, 9 brains, and blue blood.

○ ○ Colossal squids have the biggest eyes. Their eyes are about the size of basketballs.

○ ○ Under their white coats, polar bears have jet-black fur.

○ ○ Koalas have fingerprints almost identical to humans, even under a microscope.

○ ○ Bees have five eyes, two large compound eyes, and three smaller ocelli eyes in the center of their head.

○ ○ Geckos have eyes up to 350 times more sensitive to color at night than humans.

○ ○ Giraffes are missing their front teeth! Maybe they should ask Santa for them!

○ ○ Mourning geckos are all female. They are parthenogenetic, meaning that they can reproduce without male species. An egg can develop into an embryo without being fertilized by a sperm.

Find Out More!

Visit National Geographic

https://www.nationalgeographic.com/animals/

Or World Wildlife Fund

https://www.worldwildlife.org/

EXTRAORDINARY EARTH

○ ○ The speed of light is 186,287.49 miles per second or 670,616,629 mph (miles per hour), 1,079,252,848.8 (1.07 billion) km per hour. That's 11,160,000 times faster than a car on a highway.

○ ○ Sunlight takes 8 minutes and 17 seconds to travel to the Earth. If the sun exploded we wouldn't know until over 8 minutes later!

○ ○ The Earth rotates at a speed of 1,000 miles per hour or 1,674 kilometers per hour.

○ ○ The Earth orbits the sun at a speed of nearly 30 kilometers per second (18 miles per second). That's 107,826 kilometers or 67,000 miles per hour.

○ ○ You can only feel motion if your speed changes. For example, if you are in a car that is moving at a constant speed on a smooth surface, you will not feel much motion. Thus, we do not feel the movement of the Earth because its speed is constant.

○ ○ The name Earth is at least 1,000 years old. It comes from Old English, 'eor(th)e' and 'ertha', meaning "the ground."

○ ○ There are more than 326 quadrillion gallons of water on Earth.

○ ○ The highest temperature ever recorded on Earth was 136 degrees Fahrenheit (58 Celsius) in the Libyan desert. The coldest temperature ever measured was -126 Fahrenheit (-88 Celsius) at Vostok Station in Antarctica.

○ ○ The Earth weighs about 13 sextillion pounds or almost 6 sextillion kilograms. A sextillion is a thousand quintillions or a million quadrillion or a billion trillion.

○ ○ Scientists calculate the weight (mass) of the Earth using the Earth's radius and the Law of Universal Gravitation since they can't exactly put Earth on a scale.

○ ○ Earth is thought to be between 4.5 and 4.8 billion years old. The age of Earth is found by measuring the age of very old Earth rocks. This is done by measuring the rate at which elements of the radioactive metal uranium decay (break down) into lead.

It would take around 5,280 hours to drive around the Earth's equator. The Earth's circumference (the distance all the way around the equator) is 24,901 miles (40,075 kilometers). Its diameter (the distance from one side to the other through Earth's center) is 7,926 miles (about 12,756 kilometers).

Great Geography

○ ○ The Earth's Longest Mountain Range Is underwater. The Mid-Ocean Range stretches nearly 65,000 kilometers (40,390 miles) up and down the Atlantic Ocean.

○ ○ Likewise, the Earth's largest waterfall is also underwater. In the Denmark Strait cataract colder nordic waterfalls for over 3 kilometers or nearly 2 miles. This is more than three times the height of Angel Falls in Venezuela. It is also more than 130 times more voluminous than land waterfalls with 925 million gallons falling per second.

○ ○ About 95% of all life on Earth lives in the ocean.

○ ○ Scientists calculate that humans have explored only about 5% of the Earth's oceans. Since oceans cover over two-thirds of the Earth's surface, and humans have explored only 5% of the oceans, humans have not explored the majority of this planet.

○ ○ The deepest place on Earth, the Challenger Deep, is deeper than Mt. Everest put upside down. While Mt. Everest stands at 29,029 feet above sea level, Challenger Deep is 36,070 feet below sea level.

○ ○ It would take over an hour for a heavy object to sink to the bottom of Challenger Deep.

○ ○ More than one million earthquakes shake the Earth every year.

○ ○ The eruption of Krakatoa in 1883 was so loud that it was heard in Australia nearly 4,800 kilometers or almost 3,000 miles away.

○ ○ Continents shift at 1.5 centimeters (0.6 inches) a year which is about the same rate as your fingernails grow.

○ ○ Australia is wider than the moon. Australia is 4,000 kilometers or 2,485 miles from its most western point to its most eastern while the moon is 2,159.2 miles (3,475 km) in diameter.

○ ○ The Earth's greatest sheer vertical drop at 4,101 feet or 1,250 meters is Mt. Thor on Baffin Island, Canada. If you stepped off the edge of Mt. Thor, you would fall almost a mile before you hit the ground.

○ ○ In the Philippines there is a lake within an island within a lake within an island. Vulcan Point, an island within Main Crater Lake is located on Volcano Island which is located in Lake Taal, Lake Taal is located on the island of Luzon.

○ ○ The tallest mountain from its base at the bottom of the ocean to its peak is Mauna Kea at 32,808 feet. That's 3,000 feet taller than Mt. Everest.

○ ○ At 20,664 feet, Mount Chimborazo is the tallest mountain in Ecuador, and the Andes Mountains and the highest mountain in the world if you measure from the Earth's center. This is due to its location on the equatorial bulge, since the Earth is not a true sphere but is a bit squashed.

○ ○ Iceland is growing by nearly 5 centimeters annually. This is because it is divided by the North American and European tectonic plates which are growing wider apart.

○ ○ In Taylor Valley, Antarctica there is a blood-red waterfall. Blood Falls is nearly five stories tall and releases red, briny water from the Taylor Glacier.

COOL COUNTRIES

○ ○ Uganda has 11,000 species of birds and 11% of the world's bird population.

○ ○ Morocco is home to the world's oldest university. The University of Al-Karaouine dates back to 859 A.D.

○ ○ Ecuador is the first country to recognize nature rights. In 2008, it stated that nature has the "right to exist, persist, maintain and regenerate its vital cycles."

○ ○ Canada has the longest coastline on Earth at 125,000 miles or 201,168 kilometers. For comparison, the U.S. Is only 2,680 miles or 4,313 kilometers wide.

○ ○ Zimbabwe has the lowest life expectancy in the world. The average for men is 37 while it is only 34 for women.

○ ○ Cote d'Ivoire is the world's biggest producer of cocoa.

○ ○ Coffee originated in modern-day Ethiopia. Legend has it that a shepherd noticed that his sheep were exceptionally restless from eating the leaves of the coffee plants.

○ ○ Ancient Egypt gave us the first toothpaste. Made of myrrh, burnt eggshells, pumice, and burnt ashes of ox hooves, Ancient Egyptians brushed their teeth with their fingers as they had not invented the toothbrush yet.

○ ○ There is a highway in Belgium that can be seen from the moon!

○ ○ Niger is home to the largest petroglyph in the world. Created nearly 8,000 years ago, the rock carving depicts 218-foot-tall giraffes.

○ ○ The Czech Republic is the castle capital of the world with more than 2,000 castles for tourists to visit.

○ ○ The largest exporter of pepper is Vietnam. Next time you add salt and pepper to your food, you will likely have something that traveled all the way from Vietnam on your table.

○ ○ The world's oldest national park is in Mongolia. In the 18th century, the Qing Dynasty called for the protection of the Bogd Khan Mountain's natural beauty and diverse wildlife.

○ ○ Denmark has more bicycles than personal cars. Only four out of 10 Danes own a vehicle, while nine out of 10 own a bike.

○ ○ New Zealand is the first self-governing country in the world to allow women to vote in parliamentary elections.

○ ○ Liberia was founded by the American Colonization Society in the early 1800s. It was intended as a place where free-born black Americans and freed slaves could live. Nearly 20,000 people moved there in the first few years.

What country does not have a written constitution?

Answer: Great Britain

○ ○ Armenia requires students to take chess lessons. As a result, the country often wins international competitions.

○ ○ The Limbo Dance comes from Trinidad and Tobago. It was originally meant to reflect the cycle of life and was performed at funerals.

o o The only country in the world to be named after a woman is St. Lucia. French settlers gave this Caribbean island its name after Saint Lucia of Syracuse.

o o The only country in the world to be in all four hemispheres is Kiribati in the central Pacific Ocean.

o o The world's top producer of false teeth is Liechtenstein. The manufacturer, Ivoclar Vivadent, produces 60 million artificial teeth every year, which is 20% of all false teeth.

o o Tuvalu, a country of islands between Hawaii and Australia, generates most of its money from the fortuitous country domain code: .tv.

o o The smallest recognized country in the world is The Holy See (the Vatican). Although it uses the Euro, it mints its own coins and prints its own stamps.

Find Out More!

Visit CIA Factbook:

https://www.cia.gov/the-world-factbook/

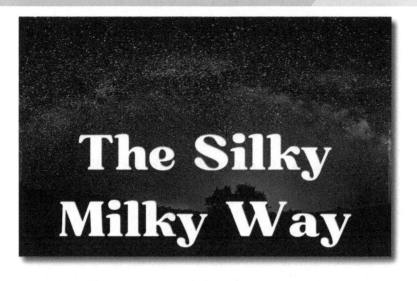

The Silky Milky Way

○ ○ The Earth is located in the Orion Arm of the galaxy the Milky Way, which is part of a group of galaxies called the Local Group which in turn is part of the Virgo Supercluster of galaxies.

○ ○ It would take 2 million years to reach the nearest large galaxy, Andromeda, traveling at the speed of light.

○ ○ If each star in the Milky Way was a grain of sand, it would fill an olympic-sized swimming pool.

○ ○ Our solar system orbits the Milky Way galaxy's center at around 827,000 kph (514,000 mph). At this rate, one could travel around the Earth's equator in 2 minutes and 54 seconds.

○ ○ If our solar system was the size of a U.S. quarter, the Milky Way would be as big as the U.S. and the sun would be a microscopic speck of dust.

○ ○ The center of the Milky Way tastes like raspberries and smells like rum. The IRAM radio telescope detected a chemical called ethyl formate which gives rum its distinct smell and raspberries their distinct flavor.

○ ○ The Milky Way measures about 120,000 light-years across.

○ ○ The Milky Way produces about seven new stars annually.

∘ ∘ The Milky Way was originally recognized as a band of individual stars by Galileo in 1620. However, Edwin Hubble discovered the Milky Way's true shape and recognized that there were even more galaxies in our universe.

∘ ∘ The Milky Way and its neighbor galaxy, Andromeda, will collide in about 4 billion years. They are crashing at a rate of 120 km per second (75 miles per second).

∘ ∘ According to a Cherokee legend, the Milky Way was formed when a dog stole a bag of cornmeal and spilled some as he was being chased. Thus the Cherokee refer to the galaxy as"The Way the Dog Ran Away".

∘ ∘ Chinese legend says the gods placed a river to keep their weaver and a herdsman who loved her apart. Therefore, the Milky Way is known as 'the silver river" in China.

∘ ∘ The Milky Way rotates around a central axis. It is believed that the Sun (and our solar system) have traveled about a third of the way around this center.

> **It would take 450 million years for a modern spacecraft to reach the center of our galaxy.**

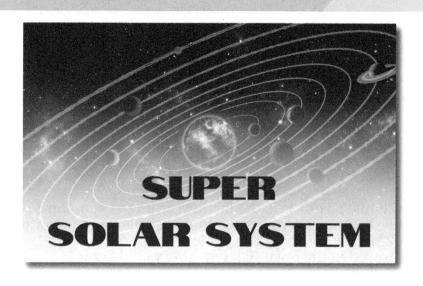

SUPER SOLAR SYSTEM

○ ○ You could fit 1 million Earths inside the sun.

○ ○ There is no such thing as moonlight. The light from the moon is simply a reflection of sunlight.

○ ○ The core of the Earth is as hot as the surface of the sun, 10,000 Fahrenheit or 5,600 Celsius.

○ ○ Footprints on the moon stay forever because there is no wind on the moon.

○ ○ While most planets in our solar system spin counter-clockwise, Venus is the only planet that spins clockwise.

○ ○ The fastest-spinning planet in our solar system is Jupiter. A day in Jupiter is only 10 hours.

○ ○ Venus has the longest day. A single rotation takes about 243 Earth days.

○ ○ Not surprisingly, Mercury, the planet closest to the sun has the shortest year. It takes 88 Earth days for Mercury to orbit the sun.

○ ○ Mercury years are shorter than Mercury days! A Mercury day is 176 Earth days. That Mercury orbits the sun twice in the time it takes for the sun to rise and set on Mercury.

∘ ∘ Neptune takes the longest to orbit the sun. A Neptunian year is 164.8 Earth years (or 60,182 Earth days).

∘ ∘ Neptune's days are only 16 hours. That means there are 89,666 Neptunian days in a Neptunian year.

∘ ∘ The hottest planet in our solar system is not the closest planet to the sun, Mercury, but rather Venus. Venus has an average surface temperature of around 450° C or 842° F.

∘ ∘ While Neptune is the farthest from the sun, the coldest planet is Uranus. Uranus recorded a temperature of -224°C or -371.2° F, the coldest temperature ever measured in the Solar System: a very chilly -224° C.

∘ ∘ The sun's mass is 99.86% of our solar system's mass.

∘ ∘ Sunsets on Mars look blue.

∘ ∘ The planet with the most volcanos is Venus with more than 1,600 major volcanoes across the surface.

∘ ∘ Jupiter has the most moons in our solar system with 92 known satellites. (It is possible Saturn has more but they haven't been counted as of yet.)

∘ ∘ From Earth, we can only see 5% of the universe.

∘ ∘ Our days are getting longer. Earth's rotation is slowing down due to the tidal effects the Moon has on the Earth's rotation.

∘ ∘ It only takes 62 miles to reach Outer Space. While there is no official border, the Kármán line, at 62 miles above sea level, is conventionally used in space treaties and aerospace records.

∘ ∘ We always see the same side of the moon. The moon orbits the Earth at the same rate it rotates on its axis therefore only ever showing one side of itself to the Earth.

∘ ∘ It rains sulfuric acid and snows metal on Venus.

∘ ∘ The moon may one day escape Earth's gravity. The moon moves 1.6 inches (4 cm) away from the Earth every year.

○ ○ Russian Cosmonaut, Valentina Tereshkova, was the first woman in space. She orbited the Earth 48 times in three days during her time in space.

○ ○ The tallest mountain in our solar system is Olympus Mons on Mars at 16 miles (25 km). This means it's nearly three times as tall as Mt. Everest.

○ ○ Uranus rotates on its side. Meaning its north pole doesn't stay on top and the side that faces the sun is always facing the sun.

○ ○ A person who weighs 220 lbs on Earth would weigh 84 lbs on Mars. Weight is someone's mass times the gravitational pull of the planet. A smaller planet, like Mars, has less gravitational pull, meaning you weigh less.

○ ○ There are 5 recognized dwarf planets in our solar system: Ceres, Makemake, Haumea, Eris, and Pluto.

What planet is the lightest?

Answer: Saturn

Unique Universe

○ ○ The Universe contains over 100 billion galaxies.

○ ○ The Universe expands by a billion miles in each direction every hour.

○ ○ There's a planet made of diamonds twice the size of the earth. The "super earth," aka, 55 Cancrie, is most likely covered in graphite and diamond.

○ ○ There are more stars in the universe than grains of sand on all the beaches on Earth. It is estimated that there are 10 to 22nd-power stars in the universe. That's a 10 with 22 zeroes after it.

○ ○ Astronomers don't count stars individually but rather estimate the number of stars by multiplying the number of stars in a galaxy by the number of galaxies.

○ ○ When stars explode, they can create a black hole. Nothing can escape the gravitational pull of a black hole.

○ ○ There is a black hole at the center of every galaxy.

○ ○ 95% of the Universe is invisible.

○ ○ The universe is 13.5 billion years old. That's three times older than our planet Earth.

○ ○ A neutron star, a star formed during a supernova, spins 600 times per second.

○ ○ Supernovas are massive stellar explosions that can be up to 10 times the size of our sun. These events are incredibly luminous and can outshine an entire galaxy.

○ ○ Neutron stars are incredibly dense, with a mass of about 2.8 times that of our sun but average only 12 miles in diameter, that's 72,000 times smaller than the sun!

○ ○ A teaspoon of neutron star material would weigh as much as a mountain on Earth.

○ ○ Neutron stars are incredibly hot, with a surface temperature of about 1 million degrees Celsius or 1.8 million degrees Fahrenheit.

○ ○ Astronomers predict that our sun will die in a supernova in about 5 billion years.

○ ○ Scientists have detected a radio signal in space from 5 billion light-years away.

○ ○ There are planets that orbit other stars. Called exoplanets, astronomers have confirmed around 4,000 of them, although there may be countless more.

○ ○ If two pieces of the same type of metal touch in space, they will merge and become one due to the lack of air and water in space.

○ ○ About 10 billion light-years away, scientists have discovered a vapor cloud that has 140 trillion times the water as all of the Earth's oceans.

Find Out More!

Visit National Aeronautics and Space Administration (NASA):

https://www.nasa.gov/

TREMENDOUS TECHNOLOGY

○ ○ There are goats at Google Headquarters in Mountain View, California. Google rents the goats to "mow" the grass and reduce carbon emissions.

○ ○ While we now carry phones with gigabytes of data in our pockets, megabytes (1024 MG is 1 GB) used to weigh hundreds of pounds.

○ ○ The first automatic computing machine was developed in 1822 by Charles Babbage, known as "the father of computers", in order to tabulate polynomials. In other words, it was a calculator that could do algebra.

○ ○ Charles Babbage designed the Analytical Engine, what would have been the first general mechanical computer. Unfortunately, due to a lack of funding, it was never built.

○ ○ Ada Lovelace, considered the world's first computer programmer, wrote an algorithm designed to be carried out by a machine before computers even existed!

○ ○ Ada Lovelace understood that computers could be used for more than just number crunching. Her insights on computing and its potential had a profound impact on the history of programming and computers.

○ ○ The first modern computer was created by Konrad Zuse in his parents' living room from 1936 to 1938.

○ ○ In 1936, the Water Integrator, a computer run on water, was created in Russia.

○ ○ In 1826, the first photograph ever taken took 8 hours to expose.

○ ○ The original Xbox had sound bites of real space missions.

○ ○ Invented by Levi Hutchins in 1787, the first alarm clock could only ring once at 4:00 a.m.

○ ○ The first vending machine was invented in 1884 by William Henry Fruen.

○ ○ In 1974, the first product with a barcode to be scanned was a packet of gum.

○ ○ Surgeons that grew up playing video games more than 3 hours per week make 37% fewer errors.

○ ○ In 1973, the first-ever cell phone call was made in New York City by Martin Cooper, who worked for Motorola.

What did the first text message say?

A. Happy Birthday!

B. Hello! How are you?

C. Where are you?

D. Merry Christmas

Answer: D Merry Christmas

○ ○ The QWERTY keyboard was originally designed to ensure slow typing. The letters are spaced so that the people using typewriters avoided jams.

○ ○ On average, there are 500,000 new internet users a day.

○ ○ More people have cell phones than toilets. There are more than 6 billion people with cell phones, however, only 4.5 billion have access to working toilets.

○ ○ As of 2022, there are 5.1 billion Internet users, and 4.5 billion of them access it on their mobile phones.

○ ○ The first website ever was posted in 1989 by British scientist Tim Berners-Lee. The website is still up as of the year of this book's publication, 2023.

○ ○ Google receives more than 99,000 searches every second.

○ ○ Artificial intelligence (AI) can now identify objects as well as humans. In a recent study, AI was able to identify objects with an accuracy of 96.3%, while humans had an accuracy of 96.5%.

○ ○ The term "computer bug" was first used in 1947 by Grace Hopper. A bug is an error in a program or system that causes it to malfunction. The first bug was found in the Harvard Mark II computer when it produced incorrect results.

○ ○ The first laptop was created in 1981 by a British computer scientist named Adam Osborne. The Osborne 1 was released in April of that year and weighed a whopping 24.5 pounds.

OUTRAGEOUS ROBOTS

○ ○ In the early 1950s, George Devol invented the first digitally operated robot named "Unimate". Although Devol attempted to market the Unimate, it was not a commercial success.

○ ○ Robots have been defusing bombs for 40 years so that humans do not have to expose themselves to explosive danger, despite what you see in action movies.

○ ○ Google X's Boston Dynamics built a four-legged robotic dog named Spot for the U.S. Marines. Spot can carry up to 400 pounds of equipment and fight in combat.

○ ○ With an aging population, the Japanese government is investing nearly a third of its budget into Care-Robots for the elderly.

○ ○ A Japanese company developed a robot named Robear, a "strong robot with a gentle touch" that has intelligent vision, flexible movement, and giant arms strong enough to lift a human right off the ground.

○ ○ SIAR, a sewage inspection robot, can navigate and inspect sewage systems so that humans do not have to.

○ ○ Farmers now can program robots to plant seeds, weed, water, and spray pesticides without needing to go into the fields.

○ ○ There are robots so small that you cannot even see them with the naked eye! Nano-robots are microscopic robots able to interact with and manipulate matter at the atomic and molecular levels. Nano-robots could be used to deliver drugs directly to cancer cells or to carry out delicate surgery without damaging healthy tissue. They could also be used to create artificial organs or to repair damaged tissue.

○ ○ Raptor, a robot designed to sprint, can run twice as fast as a human.

○ ○ Sophia, a social humanoid robot, is the first robot to be granted citizenship in any country. On October 25th, 2017 the Kingdom of Saudi Arabia gave Sophia citizenship.

○ ○ Janken, a humanoid robot with some superhuman abilities, wins rock paper scissors 100% of the time by using high-speed recognition and reaction.

○ ○ Robotic prosthetics (artificial arms and legs) can work like real human body parts by reading brain signals.

○ ○ Created as a part of Honda's research and development robotics program, Asimo cost $2.5 million to build making it the world's most expensive robot.

○ ○ Self-driving mining robots can locate rare minerals underground and prevent humans from going into dangerous mines.

○ ○ Kevin Warwick is the first self-proclaimed cyborg because he implanted computer chips in his left arm. As a result, he can remotely operate doors and gadgets connected around him.

Fascinating Food

o o An avocado contains more than twice as much potassium as a banana.

o o Broccoli has twice the vitamin C of an orange and almost as much calcium as whole milk. In addition, because of the vitamin K in broccoli, the calcium is better absorbed!

o o The only non-animal sources of vitamin D are mushrooms and sunshine.

o o There are more bacterial cells in our intestines than there are human cells in our bodies by a ratio of 10 to 1!

o o There is as much protein in raw spinach as in sirloin steak.

o o Most of an apple's nutrients are in the skin including 50% of its fiber.

o o Potatoes can help lower blood pressure due to their high amounts of Vitamin C, B6, Potassium, and Kukoamines.

o o Anxiety and depression can be alleviated with milk. Milk contains magnesium, calcium, Vitamins B & D, and theanine all of which have been found to help lower symptoms of anxiety and depression.

○ ○ There are over 50,000 different types of edible plants on the planet.

○ ○ The most consumed fruit in the world is mangoes. Mangoes are a good source of fiber, folate, and vitamins A, B6, and C.

○ ○ Bananas, tomatoes, pumpkins, watermelons, and avocados are berries.

○ ○ Digestion begins in the mouth, not in the stomach! Our saliva begins the process by breaking down the starches and fats in foods. In addition, chewing signals to the digestive tract that food is incoming.

○ ○ The word 'avocado' traces its origins to the Aztec word 'ahuacatl.' Avocados are also called 'alligator pear,' 'butter pear,' 'vegetable butter,' and 'midshipman's butter.'

○ ○ There are archaeological records of avocado use as early as 7,000 years B.C. in Peru and avocado seeds were buried with Incan mummies in 750 B.C.

○ ○ Lettuce belongs to the sunflower family.

○ ○ Doctors used to prescribe ketchup as a cure for indigestion.

○ ○ How do you know if a cranberry is ripe? Try bouncing it like a ball. A ripe cranberry will bounce.

○ ○ Mat Hand in 2001 set a record by eating 133 grapes in 3 minutes.

○ ○ The popsicle was invented by an 11-year-old. One day, little Frank Epperson left his soda drink outside overnight. Then, he began to sell them around Neptune Beach.

○ ○ Ancient Aztecs used chocolate as money.

○ ○ The country that consumes the most eggs is China.

○ ○ Russians eat caviar for breakfast. It is one of the traditional breakfast toppings served with crepe-like blini or thick oladyi pancakes.

○ ○ Carrots were originally purple in color.

○ ○ Brazilians eat cake for breakfast. A popular breakfast in Brazil consists of skillet-toasted French rolls (pão na chapa) and pingado, or warm milk served with sweetened coffee in a glass.

○ ○ Ancient Romans drank wine for breakfast.

○ ○ Marshmallows can be traced back to 2000 B.C.

○ ○ The largest marshmallow in the world weighs in at 93.10 kg or 205.2504 pounds.

○ ○ There are more than 40,000 varieties of rice.

○ ○ The Banaue Rice Terraces of the Philippines is considered as the "Eighth Wonder of the World".

○ ○ To grow 1 kg (2.2 pounds) of rice, it takes approximately 5,000 liters of water.

How many seeds are inside a pumpkin?

A. 100

B. 500

C. 2,000

D. 30,000

Answer: B 500

○ ○ The first pumpkin pies were more like soups or stews. American colonists would hollow out pumpkins and make a custard-like filling with milk, honey, and spices.

○ ○ The largest pumpkin pie was 20 feet in diameter.

○ ○ People first grew pumpkins around 5,000 to 7,000 B.C.

○ ○ In Windsor, Nova Scotia, Canada, there is a regatta where people row boats made of giant pumpkins.

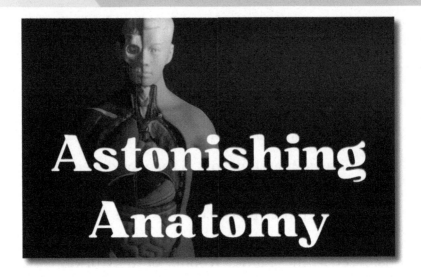

Astonishing Anatomy

○ ○ All of our muscles combined can generate about 2,000 watts of power.

○ ○ The smallest muscle in the human body is the stapedius. It is located in the ear and is responsible for dampening sound vibrations.

○ ○ The strongest muscle in the human body is the masseter. It is located in the jaw and is responsible for chewing.

○ ○ The longest muscle in the human body is the sartorius. It is located in the thigh and is responsible for leg flexion.

○ ○ The shortest muscle in the human body is the extensor digiti minimi. It is located in the hand and is responsible for extending the little finger.

○ ○ The heaviest muscle in the human body is the quadriceps. It is located in the thigh and is responsible for knee extension.

○ ○ The largest muscle in the human body is the gluteus maximus. It is located in the buttocks and is responsible for leg extension.

○ ○ Muscles can produce up to 25% of the body's heat. That's why we sometimes feel like we're "burning up" when we exercise.

○ ○ Our muscles are about 80% water. That's why it's so important to stay hydrated!

○ ○ The brain contains about 100 billion neurons. Each neuron can be connected to up to 10,000 other neurons, making the brain one of the most interconnected organs in the body. The brain has more connections than there are stars in the Milky Way Galaxy.

○ ○ The human brain can store more information than the entire Internet. According to some estimates, the average human brain has the capacity to store upwards of 2.5 petabytes of information.

○ ○ The brain can process 60,000 thoughts per day. if you had one thought every second, it would take you almost 17 hours to have 60,000 thoughts.

○ ○ Your body produces 1.5 billion cells every minute. In less than seven minutes, your body will have produced more cells than people on the planet.

○ ○ The largest bone in the human body is the femur, also known as the thigh bone.

○ ○ The smallest bone is the stirrup bone, which is located inside your ear drum.

○ ○ Your bones are stronger than steel, ounce for ounce. If you took a block of bone the size of a matchbox, it could support up to 18,000 pounds of weight.

True or False?

Babies have more bones than adults.

Answer: True

LEADING LADIES

○ ○ The world's first university, the University of al-Qarawiyyin in Morocco, was established by a woman, Fatima al-Fihri.

○ ○ Susan B. Anthony founded the National Woman Suffrage Association in 1869. Anthony was a passionate advocate for women's suffrage and she traveled across the country to give speeches. Despite her efforts, Anthony was never able to see women gain the right to vote in her lifetime.

○ ○ The American Red Cross was founded by Clara Barton in 1881. During the Civil War, Barton delivered supplies and tended to the wounded on the battlefield, earning her the nickname "Angel of the Battlefield." Through her work, she saved thousands of lives.

○ ○ Madam C.J. Walker was America's first self-made female millionaire. Daughter of slaves and orphaned at an early age, she developed her own line of hair care products for African American women. Eventually, she expanded her business to the Caribbean and Central America, opened a beauty school, and employed more than 25,000 salespeople.

○ ○ Tammy Duckworth is an inspiration to us all. Veteran and a military hero, she is the first Thai-American woman and the first disabled woman in the US Senate. Tammy Duckworth is a strong advocate for veterans and their families.

○ ○ Cleopatra was more than just a beauty, she spoke nine languages and was a savvy politician. Originally Macedonian Greek, Cleopatra was the first in her family to speak Egyptian and her rule of Egypt kept it united during turmoil and had lasting effects on the Roman Empire.

○ ○ Mary Phelps Jacobs patented the first modern bra in 1914. It quickly gained popularity, and by 1915, Jacques was selling her patents for $1,500 each. The design revolutionized women's fashion and continues to be the basis for bras today.

While Shirley Chisholm was the first Black woman elected to U.S. Congress, serving seven terms in the House of Representatives, Chisholm also became the first woman and the first Black politician to run for the president through a major political party. Nevertheless, she said:

"I want history to remember me ... not as the first Black woman to have made a bid for the presidency of the United States, but as a Black woman who lived in the 20th century and who dared to be herself."

○ ○ Empress Dowager Cixi was the de facto ruler of the Qing dynasty for 47 years. She's known for her numerous Westernization reforms, which included the Self-Strengthening Movement and the Hundred Days' Reform. She also advocated for opening China to the world, which led to the country's participation in the 1885 Berlin Conference. Cixi was a controversial figure, as she's been both praised and criticized by historians. However, there's no denying that she was a powerful and influential woman.

○ ○ Juliette Gordon Low founded the Girl Scouts in 1912. She believed that girls should be given the same opportunities as boys. With Girl Scouts, she helped girls develop their talents and skills. As a result, Gordon Low changed the way girls saw themselves and their potential.

○ ○ The first paper coffee filter was patented by a German housewife, Melitta Bentz.

○ ○ Ruth Bader Ginsburg served on the U.S. Supreme Court for over 25 years, during which time she has become known as a champion of justice. She authored influential opinions on topics such as gender equality, reproductive rights, and the death penalty.

○ ○ Temple Gradin is known for her work to improve animal welfare in the livestock industry. She developed more humane methods of slaughter that are now the industry standard. Her success did not come despite but rather because of her unique perspective as someone on the autism spectrum.

○ ○ Joan Ganz Cooney is the founder of the Children's Television Workshop and is responsible for Sesame Street and many other educational children's programs.

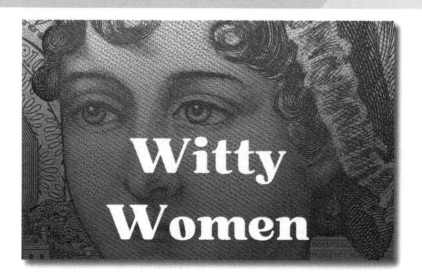

Witty Women

○ ○ Best known for her unique autobiographical writing style, Maya Angelou wrote seven autobiographies. She was also a famous Poet, dancer, singer, activist, and receiver of the Presidential Medal of Freedom by President Barack Obama in 2010.

○ ○ Sofonisba Anguissola was one of the few female artists in Renaissance Italy. She pushed the boundaries of portraiture and was commissioned to paint for wealthy families including King Phillip II of Spain.

○ ○ Not only did Jane Austen write six books before the age of 41, but her use of literary realism and free indirect narrative style also changed literature. It's easy to forget that at the time her work was experimental since now, these are standard parts of a modern-day novel.

○ ○ In order to be published, the Bronte sisters used gender-neutral pseudonyms Currer, Ellis, and Acton Bell. Their books were bestsellers and are still some of the most famous novels in English literature.

○ ○ If you like Chinese food you can thank Joyce Chen whose cookbooks have helped to popularize Chinese cuisine in the West. Chen has also been a leader in the farm-to-table movement, promoting the use of fresh, locally-grown ingredients.

○ ○ Josephine Baker was a world-famous singer and spy?!? Josephine Baker was a renowned entertainer in the 1920s and 1930s, but she was also a secret agent for the French Resistance during World War II. She would write top-secret messages in invisible ink on her sheet music.

○ ○ With her unique style of whimsy and elegance, Mary Blair left her mark on the Disney world. She was responsible for the design of some of the most iconic Disney films, such as Cinderella, Alice in Wonderland, and Peter Pan.

○ ○ Elizabeth Cochran Seaman, better known as Nellie Bly, is widely considered a pioneer in investigative journalism. Bly went undercover in 1887 to expose the conditions of the Women's Lunatic Asylum on Blackwell's Island. Bly continued to work as a journalist throughout her life, covering various topics such as women's rights, labor rights, and corruption.

○ ○ Julia Child was a world-renowned chef who broke the mold of traditional French cuisine. Julia Child began her culinary training at the Cordon Bleu in Paris. She went on to become a successful television personality and cookbook author.

True or False?

Josephine Baker would pin photos of French military installations to her underwear.

Answer: False, they were photos of German military installations. She was on the allies' side.

○ ○ Martha Gellhorn was one of the most renowned war correspondents of the 20th century. She covered conflicts in Spain, China, Finland, and many other countries. She was an advocate for human rights and helped to raise awareness of the plight of refugees.

○ ○ D. C. Fontana is a writer and producer who worked on the original Star Trek TV show. She also helped to create the Vulcan race, and she wrote the first episode featuring a Klingon. Fontana was a big advocate for diversity on the show, and she pushed for things like having a black woman as the main character. Thanks to her vision and hard work, Star Trek has became the iconic TV show that that we know today.

○ ○ Anne Frank is one of the most famous figures in Holocaust history. Anne and her family went into hiding in 1942 to avoid being sent to concentration camps. Her diary is a powerful eyewitness account of the Holocaust and has helped to bring the experiences of Jews during the Holocaust to the world's attention.

FEARLESS FEMALES

○ ○ In 1952, Virginia Apgar presented a five-step system for assessing the condition of newborn babies within a minute of birth and periodically after that. Aptly named the Apgar score, this assessment is done on newborns all over the world still today. Did you receive an Apgar score as a newborn?

○ ○ Jeanne Baret was the first woman to circumnavigate the globe. She dressed up as a man to join the crew of the Étoile voyage in the 1760s. However, she was kicked off in the French colony of Mauritius as soon as they realized she was a woman. Nevertheless, years later, she returned to France, completing the circumnavigation.

○ ○ In 1920, Bessie Colemen traveled to France to enroll in flight school because the flight schools in America did not allow non-white people, much less a Black and Native American woman to attend. She returned as both the first African American woman and the first Native-American woman in the world with a pilot's license.

○ ○ Marie Curie's research led to the discovery of radioactivity and the development of X-rays. She was the first woman to win a Nobel Prize in Physics. In addition, she was the first woman to become a professor at the University of Paris. In 1911, she won her second Nobel Prize, this time in Chemistry.

○ ○ Amelia Earhart set many aviation records. She was the first woman to fly alone at 14,000 feet, the first woman to complete a solo nonstop transcontinental flight, and the first woman to receive the Distinguished Flying Cross.

○ ○ Elizebeth Friedman broke codes, caught criminals, and helped win a world war. Friedman was a self-taught expert in cryptography and was one of the most successful codebreakers in history. She developed groundbreaking methods for breaking codes and helped the US crack the Nazis' Enigma code.

○ ○ Rosalind Franklin was a chemist and X-ray crystallographer who made critical contributions to the discovery of the structure of DNA. Franklin's work was vital to the development of the theory of complementary base pairing, which is central to our understanding of how DNA replicates itself. Unfortunately, Franklin's contributions to the field of DNA research were not recognized during her lifetime.

○ ○ In 1960, Jane Goodall began her groundbreaking field study of chimpanzees in Tanzania. Goodall's observations of chimpanzees in the wild led her to conclude that they are remarkably like humans. Goodall's work has shown that chimpanzees can make and use tools, engage in cooperative hunting, and pass on their knowledge to successive generations. Goodall has also worked to create sanctuaries for orphaned and displaced chimpanzees.

The Shark Lady

Eugenie Clark, nicknamed "the Shark Lady" was one of the world's leading experts on sharks. She was unafraid to get up close and personal with her subjects, often swimming with the sharks to better study them.

Amazing Athletics

○ ○ One of the most decorated Olympians of all time, Simone Biles has won five Olympic gold medals, fourteen World Championship medals, and countless other titles. In addition, Biles, along with fellow U.S. gymnasts like Aly Raisman, has spoken out against sexual assault and advocated for victims of sexual assault.

○ ○ Alice Coachman was the first African American woman to win an Olympic gold medal. As a Black athlete, she was not allowed to train at segregated facilities. Coachman had to make up her own routines before receiving an athletic scholarship to the Tuskegee Institute in Tuskegee, Alabama.

○ ○ In just 45 minutes, Jesse Owens set 3 world records and tied a fourth. Owens broke the world records for the 220-yard dash, the 220-yard low hurdles, and the running broad jump, and equaled the world record for the 100-yard dash.

○ ○ The fastest person on Earth is said to be determined by the 100-meter dash. Usain Bolt has an all-time record with a time of 9.58 seconds and won the 2016 Rio Olympics with a time of 9.81 seconds.

○ ○ In 2010, a Wimbledon tennis match between John Isner and Nicolas Mahut lasted 11 hours and 5 minutes. They had to play it over three days!

○ ○ Swedish Armand Duplantis set the world record for the highest pole vault at 6.18 meters (20 ft 3.3 inches). Russian Yelena Isinbayeva set the record for women at 5.06 meters (16 ft 7 inches).

○ ○ Ski ballet is a competitive sport, with athletes often performing complex tricks and flips. Developed in the 1960s, it is a combination of skiing and ballet and is often performed to music. It even featured as a demonstration sport in the Winter Olympic Games in 1988 and 1992.

○ ○ In 1963, Hall of Fame pitcher Gaylord Perry stated, "They'll put a man on the moon before I hit a home run." Nevertheless, Perry hit the first and only home run of his career, just hours after Neil Armstrong stepped onto the lunar surface.

○ ○ The "round formation huddle" in American football began because deaf quarterback Paul Hubbard needed his teammates to be close enough to interpret his signs.

○ ○ Throughout one game, soccer players will run an average of seven miles.

○ ○ The chances of making a hole-in-one are 12,500 to 1 and 2,500 to 1 for professionals.

○ ○ The Olympic rings are yellow, green, red, black, and blue because these are the colors in every flag of the world.

○ ○ Kareem Abdul-Jabbar has scored a total of 38,387 points during his career making him the all-time leading scorer in the NBA.

○ ○ The first Olympic race was won by a chef. The first Olympic race took place in 776 B.C and was won by a chef named Corubus.

○ ○ The US swimmer Michael Phelps has won a total of 23 Olympics medals, the most decorated Olympian to date.

○ ○ Table tennis balls can travel off the paddle at a speed of 105.6 mph or 169.95 kph.

○ ○ Bowling was invented around 3200 B.C. in Egypt.

○ ○ Ben Smith ran run 401 marathons in 401 days. That's 10,506 miles altogether.

○ ○ Grete Waitz won nine New York City Marathons between 1978 and 1988. She has won more NYC Marathons than anyone else.

○ ○ The USA's Connecticut Women's basketball team once won 90 games in a row. Not a single game was lost between the start of the 2008-2009 season and the end of 2010.

○ ○ In just one year, soccer legend Pele scored 127 goals. No other player has beaten that in a single year.

○ ○ Martina Navratilova set the record for the most Wimbledon wins in a row with a streak of six between 1982 and 1987.

What sport has the most participants in the world?

A. Fishing

B. Soccer

C. Tennis

D. Running

Answer: A Fishing

○ ○ At age 86, German gymnast Johanna Quaas was still competing on parallel bars and floor exercises, making her the world's oldest gymnast. You are never too old to live your dreams.

○ ○ Teresa Edwards has four gold Olympic medals and one bronze for basketball, while the top male athlete, Carmelo Anthony, only has three gold and one bronze.

○ ○ Jonathan Edwards, from the UK, set the record for the triple jump at the 1995 World Championships, jumping 18.29m.

○ ○ Limbo skating is a type of skating where the skater limbos under one or several low bars. 11-year-old Shristi Sharma, 11, limbo skated for 25 meters under bars 6.69 inches above the ground, setting the bar high for future limbo skaters.

○ ○ In just 14.65 seconds, less than the time to read this fact out loud, Ukrainian Olga Liashchuk crushed three whole watermelons between her thighs, the fastest time ever recorded.

○ ○ Minoru Yoshida from Japan in 1980 set the world record for the most consecutive push-ups with 10,507 push-ups in a row.

WACKY WEDDINGS

o   o Couples in the Congo must not smile on their wedding day to demonstrate how serious they take the occasion.

o   o In Fiji, men must ask for their future bride's hand by giving a sperm whale's tooth, called a tabua, to their future father-in-law.

o   o German guests break porcelain for the couple to sweep up in the first bit of housekeeping they must do together. Then, they are often presented with a large log. To prove they can do difficult tasks together, the couple must see the log together.

o   o To promote fertility in the Czech Republic, an infant is placed on the bed of the bride and groom before they are married.

o   o Newlyweds in Russia bite into a special sweet bread called "karavay" without using their hands. Whoever takes the biggest bite is the head of the family.

o   o In India, on the wedding day, the bride's family will steal the groom's shoes and hold them for ransom.

o   o At wedding receptions in Niger, the entertainment is a camel that dances!

o   o At the end of the 1400s in Venice, diamond rings were given as betrothal gifts among the elite.

○ ○ At Peruvian wedding receptions, there is a cake for the bridesmaids. Inside the cake are charms attached to ribbons, one of them being a fake wedding ring. At the party, each single women pull on a ribbon. The woman who gets the fake wedding ring will be married next.

○ ○ The first recorded evidence of marriage ceremonies uniting one woman and one man dates from about 2350 B.C., in Mesopotamia.

○ ○ A Jewish wedding in Jerusalem in 1993 was the largest wedding where 30,000 people attended.

○ ○ A wedding in Dubai was the most expensive wedding in the world costing $22 million American dollars.

○ ○ The longest wedding dress train measured over 515 feet or 157 meters.

○ ○ To sweeten their union, Greeks put a sugar cube in their sleeve on their wedding day.

○ ○ According to Hindu tradition, it is good luck to have rain on your wedding day.

○ ○ To purify themselves, Moroccan brides bathe in milk before the wedding ceremony.

○ ○ Queen Victoria's wedding cake weighed 300 pounds or 136 kilograms.

Birthday Bashes

○ ○ In both Jamaica and Brazil, friends and family will cover the birthday person in flour. In Jamaica, they call this "antiquing". In Brazil, they will sometimes also egg them.

○ ○ In Canada, in order to ward off bad luck, people will smear butter on the birthday person's nose. This is sometimes referred to as "greasing."

○ ○ If you want to live a long life in China, you eat extra-long noodles on your birthday. Called "longevity noodles", they symbolize, you guessed it, a long life. According to tradition, each strand should be eaten whole, you cannot break it before you eat it.

○ ○ Our birthdays don't actually count the day we were born, but rather the anniversary of our birth. However, in Korea, your first birthday is the actual birth date. Thus, your age in Korea would be a year older.

○ ○ Koreans eat seaweed soup for their birthdays to honor their mothers who ate it as part of their postpartum recovery.

○ ○ Ancient Egyptians were the first to celebrate "birthdays" celebrating the birth of Gods when Pharaohs were crowned.

○ ○ Ancient Greeks were the first to put candles on a cake to celebrate Artemis, the goddess of the moon.

○ ○ Heard of the gingerbread man? What if he was a birthday cake? Danish children get large cakes in the shape of men and women decorated with candies, icing, and chocolate.

○ ○ In the 1700s, Germans began celebrating Kinderfeste where they would put one candle for each year of life. The birthday child got to make a wish while blowing out the candles.

○ ○ The Happy Birthday song started as the song "Good Morning to All" composed by a kindergarten teacher, Mildred Hill in 1893.

○ ○ You may know the Mexican tradition of hitting a piñata full of candy, however, it is also customary to wake up the birthday person at midnight with a mariachi group singing "Las Mañanitas" or the little mornings.

In what country do they rub yogurt on a birthday person's forehead?

A. Germany

B. Nepal

C. Japan

D. Canada

Answer: B Nepal

Terrific Traditions

○ ○ La Tomatina is a food festival in Valencia, Spain that attracts around 50,000 participants from all over the world. The festival consists of a week-long celebration which culminates in a tomato battle on the final day.

○ ○ The Monkey Buffet Festival held annually in Lopburi, Thailand celebrates and honors the thousands of macaques at the Phra Prang Sam Yot temple. Monkeys are treated to a buffet of fruits, vegetables, and other monkey-friendly foods.

○ ○ The Air Guitar World Championships are the ultimate battle of the bands, held annually in Oulu, Finland. The competition is judged on technique, stage presence, and overall rockitude.

○ ○ Śmigus Dyngus, also known as Wet Monday, is a Polish celebration that takes place on Easter Monday. Today, the holiday is celebrated with water being thrown on friends and strangers alike. Those who get soaked the most are said to be the luckiest in love.

○ ○ Nyepi is a New Year's celebration in Bali that is a time to reflect on the past year and set intentions for the new one. For 24 hours, everyone on the island agrees to stay inside and make as little noise as possible.

○ ○ It is a tradition in Rio de Janeiro to get into the water and jump over seven waves and make seven wishes on New Year's Day.

○ ○ Yi Peng is a festival of lights that is celebrated in Thailand. During Yi Peng, people release lanterns into the sky. The lanterns are made of paper and have a small candle inside them. Yi Peng is a time to celebrate new beginnings and let go of negative energy.

○ ○ The Wife-Carrying World Championships is an annual event held in Finland. Like it sounds, the race consists of a husband and wife team completing an obstacle course while the wife is carried by the husband.

○ ○ Instead of putting their tooth under their pillow for the tooth fairy, Greek children throw their teeth onto the roof for good luck and healthy teeth.

○ ○ The Albuquerque International Balloon Fiesta is the world's largest hot-air balloon festival. The festival takes place over nine days in October and up to 100 hot air balloons take to the skies each morning and evening during the festival.

○ ○ The Fuji Shibazakura Festival is a spring spectacle in Japan south of Lake Motosuko. Fields of pink moss bloom with Mount Fuji in the background. Visitors come from all over the world to see the beautiful display.

In what city is the world's largest hot-air balloon festival?

A. Albuquerque, New Mexico

B. Houston, Texas

C. San Francisco, California

D. Vancouver Canada

Answer: A Albequerque

TOWERING TREES

○ ○ It is estimated that 80% of the Earth's forests have already been destroyed through deforestation by humans.

○ ○ Dating back 250 million years, one of the oldest living tree species is Ginkgo biloba.

○ ○ A baobab tree can store up to 120,000 liters of water in its swollen trunk.

○ ○ The tallest trees in the world are the California redwoods.

○ ○ An average size tree can provide enough wood to make 170,100 pencils.

○ ○ Ancient Egyptians made aspirin from the bark of the willow tree.

○ ○ The tallest tree ever was an Australian eucalyptus. In 1872 it measured 435 feet tall.

○ ○ Trees are made up of 99% dead cells. The only parts of the tree that are living are parts of the leaves, root tips, and the phloem (a thin layer of under bark).

○ ○ A bonsai orange tree will actually produce tiny oranges.

o o The heaviest tree in the world is a whole forest of quaking aspen in Utah, which is actually one single tree   It weighs 6,000,000 Kg. or 13,227,735 pounds.

o o Only a handful of scientists, sworn to secrecy, know the locations of the oldest tree in the world, Methuselah, and the tallest tree in the world, Hyperion.

o o The smallest tree is the dwarf willow. Also known as the Salix Herbacea, it typically grows only 2 inches high with round, shiny green leaves.

o o Native to southern North America, and northern South America, the manchineel is the world's most dangerous tree, sometimes known as poison guava or beach apple, it grows on coastal beaches.   Every part of the tree contains toxins that can cause blisters and skin breakouts on human skin just from the touch. Blindness can also occur if it touches a person's eyes.

o o The longest-living organisms on Earth are bristlecone pine trees. The oldest pine is estimated to be more than 4,800 years old, meaning that that pine tree was alive when wooly mammoths roamed the Earth.

o o Planting trees and shrubs strategically can reduce your energy costs by up to 25%. A shade tree can cool your home off by as much as 20 degrees Fahrenheit or around 11 degrees Celsius on a hot summer day.

o o Trees can communicate in order to defend themselves and their neighbors from attacking insects. Willow trees, for example, emit certain chemicals when they're attacked by webworms, thereby alerting neighboring trees that there are webworms.

o o An adult tree is able to absorb more than 48 pounds of carbon dioxide annually. The tree photosynthesizes the carbon dioxide, sunlight, and water into simple sugars while releasing oxygen back into the air.

o o There are more than 60,000 known tree species on Earth.

o o Before trees, there were fungi that grew 26 feet fall on Earth.

Powerful Plants

○ ○ More than 70,000 plants are used for medicine, both traditional and modern.

○ ○ We have only studied 1% of the rainforest plants for medicinal potential. Maybe the cure for cancer is in there!

○ ○ More than two-thirds of plants are in danger of extinction.

○ ○ The elephant grass found in Africa is called that because elephants can hide in it as it can grow up to 4.5 meters or nearly 15 feet high.

○ ○ Pope Nicholas III in the Vatican City founded the first certified botanical garden in 1278 A.D.

○ ○ Coffee plants protect themselves from pests with caffeine in their tissues.

○ ○ 85% of plant life is found in the ocean!

○ ○ The Poison Garden at England's Alnwick Garden has over 100 deadly plants including hemlock, belladonna, and monkshood.

○ ○ According to plant biologist Daniel Chamovitz, plants can feel, see, smell, and remember.

○ ○ 26% of plant life on Earth is grass.

○ ○ The world's most venomous plant, gympie, is also called the "Suicide Plant". This is because it is capable of delivering a sting like "being burned with hot acid and electrocuted at the same time". Its pain is so unbearable that people have killed themselves after touching it. Gympie is a member of the nettle family.

○ ○ There are 1,700 species of plants in the Arctic tundra.

○ ○ In 2012, Russian scientists were able to grow a 32,000-year-old extinct Siberian Campion plant from seeds found in prehistoric squirrel burrows. Siberian permafrost preserved these seeds.

○ ○ Dawsonia is the tallest moss in the world, growing to 23.6" in height. It is commonly found in New Zealand, Australia, and New Guinea.

○ ○ The Mistletoe Cactus is the only cactus out of 1,750 cacti species, naturally found outside America.

○ ○ The world's smallest seeds are only 1/300th of an inch (85 micrometers) long. Epiphytic orchid seeds are so small that they are not visible to the naked eye.

○ ○ The largest seed in the world, the coco de mer, is a foot long and weighs 18 kg or nearly 40 pounds.

○ ○ Discovered in 2009, a pitcher plant in the Philippines is known to devour rats whole.

○ ○ The Great Barrier Reef is the largest living structure on Earth at over 2000 kilometers long.

FANTASTIC FLOWERS

○ ○ Vanilla beans come from the pod of an orchid, Vanilla planifolia.

○ ○ In the 1600s, tulip bulbs were worth more than gold in Holland.

○ ○ The world's biggest flower is the rafflesia. Also known as the monster flower. They are native to Sumatra, Indonesia, Malaysia, and Thailand and can reach a width of over three feet or around one meter.

○ ○ The tallest flower in the world, Titan Arum, can be up to ten feet tall and three feet wide, and it can weigh up to 24 pounds! It has a distinctive smell of rotting flesh, that's why it is also known as the "corpse flower."

○ ○ The smallest flowering plant in the world is the Asian watermeal at 0.1–0.2 mm (0.004–0.008 in) in diameter, about the size of a grain of rice.

○ ○ The first records of edible flowers date back to 140 B.C.

○ ○ Sunflowers follow the path of the sun from the east to the west.

○ ○ Moonflowers are called that because they are closed during the day, but open up and bloom during the night.

○ ○ There are more than 400,000 types of flowering plants in the world.

○ ○ The most expensive flower ever sold cost $200,000. Bought at an auction, a Shenzhen Nongke Orchid took eight years to develop and blooms once every four to five years.

○ ○ Chocolate cosmos are called that because they actually smell like chocolate.

○ ○ The color of hydrangeas is determined by the acidity level of the soil. If the soil is less acidic the flower will be pink, and the more acidic the soil, the bluer the flower.

○ ○ The agave, used to make tequila, will stay dormant for years and only blooms once and then dies.

○ ○ The largest flower auction in the world auctions 20 million flowers a day in Aalsmer, Holland.

○ ○ It is estimated that since 1750 about 57% of species of flowers have already gone extinct, and today an additional 25% of flower species are at risk of extinction.

○ ○ Roses are related to apples, raspberries, cherries, peaches, plums, nectarines, pears, and almonds.

○ ○ The world's most expensive spice, saffron, comes from the stigma of a type of crocus flower. It takes the stigma of hundreds of crocus flowers to make the spice, which is why it is so expensive.

Find Out More!

Visit the Botanical Society of America

https://botany.org/home/resources/
suggested-botanical-web-sites.html

Unbelievable Vehicles

○ ○ The first submarine was built in 1620 by Cornelius Jacobszoon Drebbel, a Dutch engineer and scientist.

○ ○ The first use of submarines in warfare was during the American Civil War. Both the Union and the Confederate sides built submarines.

○ ○ The U.S. Navy's Ohio-class nuclear submarines can stay submerged for up to three months.

○ ○ The deepest a submarine has ever been is 8,400 meters (27,560 feet).

○ ○ The largest submarine in the world is the Russian Typhoon-class nuclear submarine. Typhoon-class submarines are the largest submarines ever built, with a length of 170 meters (560 ft) and a beam of 23 meters (75 ft). The displacement of the Typhoon class is more than 48,000 tonnes (470,000 long tons; 530,000 short tons).

○ ○ There are an estimated 400 nuclear submarines in the world.

○ ○ The first hovercraft was built in 1955 by British engineer Christopher Cockerell. A hovercraft is a vehicle that can travel over land and water on a cushion of air that is being blasted downward (hovering over the air).

○ ○ The world's largest hovercraft is the Russian-built Zubr, which can carry 500 people.

○ ○ Hovercraft can reach speeds of up to 150 mph. Hovercraft are used for transportation, rescue missions, and military operations.

○ ○ The first cars didn't have steering wheels. Instead, they were steered by a tiller, which was a lever that was attached to the front wheels.

○ ○ The first cars were steam-powered and were invented in the early 1800s.

○ ○ The world's first car with an internal combustion engine was built in 1885 by Karl Benz. It was a three-wheeled vehicle that could reach a speed of 10 mph.

○ ○ The world's fastest street-legal car is the Bugatti Veyron Super Sport. It can reach a top speed of 268 miles per hour.

○ ○ Lamborghini's Veneno is not only one of the most expensive cars in the world but also one of the most exclusive. Just three were made, and each one cost a whopping $4.5 million.

○ ○ The world's longest car is the Cadillac One. It's a massive stretch limousine that's over 30 feet long.

○ ○ The world's heaviest car is the Rolls-Royce Phantom IV. At nearly three tons, this behemoth is nearly twice as heavy as the average car on the road today. Rolls-Royce only ever made 18 of these cars, and all of them were built for Heads of State or members of royalty.

○ ○ On December 17, 1903, the Wright brothers made history with the first powered flight of their Wright Flyer staying in the air for 12 seconds and covering 120 feet.

○ ○ The largest airplane in the world is the Antonov An-225 Mriya, which has a wingspan of 88.4 meters (290 feet).

○ ○ Regular commercial airline service began in 1914 with flights between St. Petersburg and Tampa, Florida.

JURASSIC JUGGERNAUTS

○ ○ The last known wooly mammoth died just 4,000 years ago. Meaning there were wooly mammoths when there were humans.

○ ○ Wooly mammoths were over 10 feet (approximately 3 meters) tall at the shoulder and weighed up to 6 tons.

○ ○ Prehistoric giant sloths, Megatheria, were enormous and weighed around 8,800 pounds or 3,990 kilograms.

○ ○ The Megalodon, a giant shark that lived in the oceans during the Miocene and Pliocene epochs, could grow to be over 60 feet long and weigh up to 100 tons. The Megalodon was the largest predator that ever lived.

○ ○ The Quetzalcoatlus, a prehistoric flying reptile had a wingspan of up to 36 feet! That's bigger than some airplanes! It is one of the largest known flying animals of all time.

○ ○ Argentinosaurus was so big that it's thought that it may have been too big to walk, and instead may have moved around by crawling on its belly! This herbivore lived during the Cretaceous period and was the largest land animal that has ever lived, with some estimates putting its length at over 100 feet!

○ ○ Meganeura monyi, a prehistoric giant dragonfly, had a wingspan of up to two and a half feet or almost one meter.

○ ○ Not all prehistoric creatures were giants. On the other end of the spectrum, there were creatures like the minuscule shrew, which weighed in at less than an ounce.

○ ○ Gigantopithecus is an extinct ape that lived in Asia from roughly 9 million to 100,000 years ago. The largest Gigantopithecus specimen ever found is a jawbone, which suggests that this ape could have reached a height of up to 10 feet (3 meters).

○ ○ Spinosaurus aegyptiacus, a massive theropod dinosaur, was up to 50 feet (around 15 meters) long and weighed up to 20 tons. It lived during the Late Cretaceous period, approximately 145-65 million years ago. Spinosaurus was one of the largest land predators that ever lived and may have been able to eat large dinosaurs.

○ ○ Titanoboa, a prehistoric snake, lived during the Paleocene epoch and could grow to be up to 50 feet (around 15 meters) long. Titanoboa is the largest snake that has ever been discovered and would have been a top predator in its ecosystem.

○ ○ Before the ancestors of homo sapiens walked the earth, another hominin lineage called paranthropus roamed Africa. Paranthropus is thought to be an ancestor of the homo genus and is sometimes referred to as a "missing link" between apes and humans.

○ ○ The Tyrannosaurus rex was the largest land predator of its time. It had a massive head with enormous teeth. It had short, stocky legs and huge claws. It could grow up to 40 feet (12 meters) long and weigh up to 7 tons.

○ ○ The Dreadnoughtus was a massive herbivorous dinosaur that lived during the Late Cretaceous period, around 77 to 65 million years ago. It is thought to have been around 85 feet (26 meters) long and 65 feet (20 meters) tall and is one of the largest land animals that has ever been discovered. This animal would have been able to consume up to 440 pounds (200 kilograms) of vegetation per day.

∘ ∘ Ambulocetus was a massive prehistoric sea creature, an early ancestor of whales, and could grow up to 50 feet long.

∘ ∘ A giant prehistoric millipede called arthropleura was the largest land invertebrate that ever lived, growing up to 8 feet long.

∘ ∘ The brachiosaurus was one of the largest dinosaurs that ever lived. This gigantic creature could grow up to 82 feet long and weigh over 80 tons!

∘ ∘ A new study of smilodon or saber tooth tigers fossils suggests that these so-called "fearsome beasts" may have actually been gentle giants. Researchers analyzed teeth marks on smilodon bones and found that they were primarily caused by play, not by fighting or hunting.

At 82 feet long and weighing over 80 tons, what is the biggest dinosaur to have ever lived?

A. Tyrannasaurus Rex

B. Argentinosaurus

C. Dreadnoughtus

Answer: D Brachiosaurus

Stunning History

○ ○ An estimated 100 hundred billion people have lived since the beginning of human life on Earth.

○ ○ Genghis Khan built the largest land empire on Earth, conquering most of Asia and parts of Europe.

○ ○ The Black Death, or the bubonic plague, was one of the deadliest pandemics in human history. In the 14th century, it killed 75 to 200 million people worldwide.

○ ○ Gunpowder was invented by the Chinese in the 9th century. It was used in warfare for the first time in the Song dynasty.

○ ○ The Taj Mahal is a mausoleum complex in India that was built under Mughal Emperor, Shah Jahan, in memory of his late wife Mumtaz Mahal.

○ ○ The Great Wall of China is the world's longest man-made structure, spanning over 13,000 miles.

○ ○ Over a million people died during the construction of the Great Wall of China.

○ ○ Originally painted in bright colors, the Terracotta Warriors, were created to protect the tomb of China's first emperor. More than 8,000 soldiers, horses, and chariots have been found at the site.

○ ○ Juneteenth is an annual commemoration of the end of slavery in the United States. Today, Juneteenth is celebrated across the country, with events and festivities that focus on African American culture and history.

○ ○ Built in 1887 in Paris, France, the Eiffel Tower was the tallest man-made structure in the world for 41 years.

○ ○ The Trail of Tears is the Cherokee name for the forced relocation of approximately 60,000 native Americans by the United States government to Indian Territory. between 1830 and 1850. The relocation of people of the "Five Civilized Tribes to Oklahoma started with the enactment of the Indian Removal Act in 1830 by Congress. Cherokee authorities estimate that 6,000 native Americans died on the 1,200-mile forced march.

○ ○ Cinco de Mayo celebrates the 1862 victory of Mexican military forces over Napoleon III's French forces in the Mexican battle for independence at Puebla.

○ ○ Ancient Egyptians believed that gold was the sweat of the sun god Ra.

○ ○ Tanks, poison gas, zeppelins, and submarines were used for the first time during World War 1.

○ ○ The ancient Egyptians were some of the first people to use makeup. Egyptians also invented perfume.

○ ○ The first human civilization emerged in Mesopotamia around 4500 B.C.

○ ○ The first city on record, Uruk, was founded by the Sumerians in 4500 B.C.

○ ○ By 3000 B.C., the Babylonians had emerged as the dominant civilization in Mesopotamia.

○ ○ The first Egyptian dynasty was founded by Narmer in 3100 B.C.

○ ○ The first dynasty of China was founded by the Xia people in 2100 B.C.

○ ○ The first civilization in the Americas was the Olmec civilization, which emerged in 1200 B.C.

○ ○ The first kingdom in Europe was the Kingdom of Mycenae, which was founded in 1600 B.C.

○ ○ The Nubian civilization was one of the earliest cultures in Africa. Archeological evidence shows that the Nubians were living in the Sudanese region by 8000 B.C. In ancient times, Nubia was known as the "Land of Gold" because of its vast reserves of precious metal. Likewise, it was also home to a number of other valuable resources, including iron, copper, and incense. Nubia was therefore a very wealthy kingdom, and its people were able to create a sophisticated society with its own unique culture.

○ ○ The Nubian pyramids are located in present-day Sudan. They are among the largest and best-preserved pyramids in the world.

○ ○ Built in the 15th century, Machu Picchu was deserted by the time the Spanish conquistadors arrived in the 16th century. It is unclear why it was built or why it was abandoned.

○ ○ The Japanese word "kamikaze" means "divine wind" and was chosen to signify the suicide pilots' belief that they were on a divine mission.

○ ○ The Kamikaze were Japanese pilots who flew their planes into enemy ships in an effort to sink them. Over 3,000 Kamikaze pilots sacrificed themselves in the war, managing to sink over 300 enemy ships.

True or False?

Sudan has around 200 pyramids twice that of Egypt.

Answer: True

Your RANDOM FACTS

Did you hear another mind-boggling fact from a friend or family member? Did you learn something from your own research that blew you away? Make your own chapter of unbelievable facts here!

○ ○ _____
_____
_____

○ ○ _____
_____
_____

○ ○ _____
_____
_____

○ ○ _____
_____
_____

Conclusion

Wowee! That was a lot of facts! Do you feel smarter? More knowledgable? Hopefully, you feel more inquisitive. Ideally, this sparked your curiosity to find out more. Don't just finish this book, put it down and forget about it forever. What facts stood out to you? What areas interested you the most? What facts were the most unknown to you? What topics did you already know the most about? I sincerely hope this book awakened a thirst for knowledge that helps you become the next Eugenie Clark, aka the Shark Lady, or Marie Curie. Find out facts about this world that no one has ever discovered before. So go out there, be bold, be brave and stun the world with more unbelievable facts yet to be uncovered by an inquisitive kid!

Made in the USA
Las Vegas, NV
09 June 2023

73182912R00050